Introduction

The philosopher Francis Bacon once said, 'We are not living in eternity. We have only this moment, sparkling like a star in our hand.' Mindfulness teaches us to see the joy and wonder in each sparkling moment of our lives, to appreciate them while they're happening and let go of the worries about the past and the future that we carry around with us. Let this book guide you along the path to finding a little more serenity and a little less stress in your life, from rising to greet the day with positivity and joy to your last thoughts of gratitude before you drift off into a peaceful night's sleep.

A NEW DAY BEGINS

What a benediction is this fragrance of the early morning!

SARAH SMILEY

As you wake up,
think about
the things you can hear,
feel or smell before
opening your eyes
- a bird singing outside, a
gentle breeze
through the window or the
smell of clean sheets.

Before you get
out of bed,
stretch your body
fully to waken
your muscles and
prepare yourself
for the day ahead.

Start your day with a minute's meditation. Repeat this mantra, focussing on its message:

'Today will be filled with positivity and joy.'

As you wash,
pay attention to
the warmth
of the water and
the scent
of your shower gel
or soap as it
cleanses
your skin.

Pick your outfit for the day carefully – remember: *soft colours and fabrics* will help promote a *feeling of serenity within.*

Make time for a
nutritious and fulfilling
breakfast. Fresh fruit and
wholegrains make a
perfect start
to the day.

Before leaving the house, *close your eyes, straighten your spine* and take several *deep breaths,* allowing the air to fill your lungs fully. Step out standing tall and *full of happiness.*

Allow yourself a little extra time to take a gentle stroll in a quiet, *calming space* before heading to work. *Let your mind wander* as you take in the beautiful colours of nature and allow the morning air to *revive you.*

Avoid checking your
phone or emails until you
have reached work.
*Let the morning
be a time of peace
and tranquillity.*

Choose to make today
a 'no rush' day.
Handle each of
your activities with the
care and attention
they deserve.

As you go about your morning activities, say these words quietly to yourself:

'I am at peace.'

HABITS FOR DAILY MINDFULNESS

You must live in the present, launch yourself on every wave, find your eternity in each moment.

HENRY DAVID THOREAU

Mix up your daily routine by taking a *different route* from your usual one. Notice how much more you *appreciate your environment* when you give your mind new sights to take in.

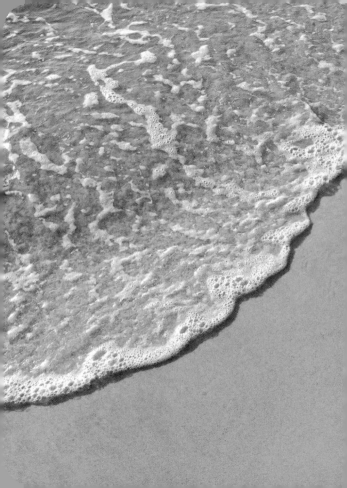

Make time in your day to *simply be.* Concentrate on your breath, and bring your thoughts back to your breathing when they *start to wander.*

Smile. Make sure you
embrace
any opportunity
today to express your
cheerfulness.

Be mindful of the words
you use today. Make a
conscious effort
to speak from a place of
love and acceptance.

If you spend most of your day sitting down, make it *part of your routine* to get up and move your body – stretching or going for a short walk can help *revive your energy levels.*

If you find yourself
feeling anxious or dwelling
on negative thoughts,
*close your eyes
and picture your
favourite place.*
Allow your mind to be
soothed by the image.

Practise mindful eating. Instead of reaching straight for a biscuit with your coffee or tea, *listen to your body.* Are you actually hungry or are you acting out of habit? *What does your body need?*

When you're carrying out daily chores, such as washing up after a meal, *practise bringing your whole awareness to the activity.*

Set aside a period of time, perhaps an hour while you prepare and eat your evening meal, where you are completely *disconnected* from the outside world. Turn off your phone, TV and laptop and use the time instead to *refocus and reconnect with yourself.*

Experience each moment as it happens. Focus on filling the present with *serenity and peace.*

Make an effort to
spend time outside
every day. Let the
natural light
brighten your mood,
and soak up the
radiance
of the sun.

POSITIVE
THINKING

If we will take the good
we find, asking no
questions, we shall have
heaping measures.

RALPH WALDO EMERSON

Start a daily
gratitude journal,
listing all the
positive things
in your life.
Notice all the
small things that
make you smile,
as well as the
bigger things to be
grateful for,
such as your health
or your family.

Notice your tendencies towards anxiety for the future or regret about the past. *Be conscious* of how they take your *awareness away from the present moment,* and rob you of time.

Practise active
listening, devoting your
whole attention
to a friend or colleague the
next time they want to talk
to you. Try not to make
instant judgements;
instead, hear them
out before calmly
thinking over
what they have said.

Know that you don't
always have to
*pay attention to
your thoughts*
or react to them –
sometimes they're simply the
chatter in your mind.

Whenever you start to feel negative emotions, take it as an opportunity to *learn about yourself.* What thought patterns are causing these emotions? How do you best overcome them?

Repeat this to yourself whenever you feel anxious, frustrated or sad:

'I flow from a place of grace.'

If you have a negative thought or reaction to something today, *take a step back* and examine why you might have responded this way. You have the *power over your thoughts.*

Turn inconvenient
moments in your day into
***opportunities for
mindfulness.***
If you're stuck in a queue
or a traffic jam, bring your
attention to how your
***body, posture and
thoughts are affected
by the situation.***

Find ways that you can be of service to the people around you. Take pleasure in *spreading goodwill and making a big difference with a small action,* such as helping somebody with their shopping or holding a door for someone.

Open your
heart and soul
to forgiveness,
both for yourself and others.
Holding on to resentment
or anger only fuels other
negative emotions.
Be open to healing
and love.

Find a shell, flower
or stone and
focus on its intricacies.
Marvel at how the
natural world produces
such beauty.

Take pleasure in the
simple things:
appreciate a child's smile
or the laughter of a friend,
and connect to the joy
that is all around you.
*Seek to expand
your heart,*
not your possessions.

Surround yourself with images that make you *feel happy and calm.* Postcards on the fridge or a photo on your desk of a *blooming flower or a beautiful beach* will give you a boost throughout the day.

STRESS-FREE LIVING

The time to be happy is now, The place to be happy is here.

ROBERT G. INGERSOLL

Body contact releases oxytocin, which can *reduce stress hormones* and help to elevate your mood. Share a *warm hug* with your loved ones or a family pet for instant *stress relief.*

Burn incense or aromatherapy oils and breathe in their *cleansing aromas* as they clear the air around you.

Exercise not only
makes you strong and
healthy, it can also
relieve tension
in the body and
boost your mood
for hours afterwards. Go
for an invigorating run,
swim or bike ride to
release any
built-up stress.

Find somewhere you can sit and be calm; overlooking a peaceful stream or pond perhaps, or gazing out over all the houses from a hillside.

When faced with a tough or trying situation, *take a moment* before reacting. Know that you have a choice in *how to respond.*

Escape the stress of mess by cleaning and organising the spaces around you. Donate your unwanted things to charity.

Your new, bright and airy surroundings will help you keep a clear mind.

Practising yoga has helped people *relieve stress* for centuries. Find a local class or buy a DVD you can follow at home to discover this *relaxing and fulfilling exercise.*

Let go of
past arguments or
disharmonies in your life.
Now is the time to move
on and focus on what
you can do today to
realign yourself.

When external
distractions threaten to
throw you off balance,
*choose to be still
and connect to your
inner peace.*

Remember, it is OK to say 'no'. Refraining from over-committing ourselves allows us to be free of a lot of *unnecessary stress and guilt.*

At the end of
your working day,
make a list
of your tasks for
tomorrow, putting the
top priorities first. You
can then turn off your
'*work mind*'
and allow yourself to
relax for the evening.

Put some fun into your schedule. Making time to *do the things we enjoy,* such as painting, reading, walking or catching up with friends is an *important part of a balanced life.*

WITH THE SETTING OF THE SUN

Each morning sees
some task begin,
each evening
sees it close;
Something attempted,
something done,
has earned a
night's repose.

HENRY WADSWORTH
LONGFELLOW

Recognise the day's *successes and achievements.* Allow yourself time to *reflect and celebrate* them before rushing on to new tasks.

Relish every bite
of your evening meal,
taking your time to
appreciate the
tastes and textures
of the food you
have prepared.

Treat yourself
to a luxurious bath,
complete with bath oils,
scented candles and
relaxing music. Enjoy the
warm water and pay
special attention
to how all your senses
are reacting to this
calming environment.

Make your bedroom a
haven for sleep
by investing in blackout
blinds, and leaving a
window open at night
to ensure you have
fresh air to keep
you cool.

Keep all electronic
devices out of your
bedroom to make sure you
associate your bed with
rest and sleep.

Turn off all sources
of artificial light
before you sleep,
including little LEDs
or blinking lights.

Make brushing your teeth
your daily reminder to
take care of yourself,
and be kind to
your body.
Take your time and do
a thorough job.

Place a handkerchief
scented with a few drops
of lavender oil under
your pillow to ensure
a restful night's sleep.

Treat your body to *seven or eight hours' sleep every night;* it has worked hard all day and needs plenty of time to *replenish its stores.*

When you are ready for bed,
breathe deeply,
releasing all the tension in
your body and all of the
day's negativity and stress.
*Breathe in serenity
and calm.*

If you're interested in
finding out more about our
books, find us on Facebook
at **Summersdale Publishers** and
follow us on Twitter at
@Summersdale.

www.summersdale.com